D1406794

MAR   2014

ANIMAL SUPERPOWERS

WHALE SHARKS
Bulletproof!

Emma Carlson Berne

PowerKiDS
press

New York

Published in 2014 by The Rosen Publishing Group, Inc.
29 East 21st Street, New York, NY 10010

First Edition

Editor: Joanne Randolph
Book Design: Kate Vlachos

Photo Credits: Cover Krzysztof Odziomek/Shutterstock.com; pp. 4, 11 iStockphoto/Thinkstock; p. 5 dive-hive/Shutterstock.com; p. 6 Monica and Michael Sweet/Flickr/Getty Images; p. 7 (sidebar) DJ Mattaar/Shutterstock.com; p. 7 rm/Shutterstock.com; p. 8 WaterFrame/Getty Images; p. 9 © iStockphoto.com/Giovanni Banfi; p. 9 © iStockphoto.com/stevedeneef; pp. 12–13 © iStockphoto.com/Krzysztof Odziomek; p. 14 Daniela Dirscherl/WaterFrame/Getty Images; p. 15 Robert Arnold/Taxi/Getty Images; p. 16 Asianet-Pakistan/Shutterstock.com; p. 17 Tatiana Ivkovich/Shutterstock.com; p. 19 Shane Gross/Shutterstock.com; p. 20 © Stock Connection/SuperStock; p. 21 (sidebar) tagstiles.com - S. Gruene/Shutterstock.com; p. 22 tororo reaction/Shutterstock.com.
Interactive eBook Only: p. 4 VideoBlocks.com ; p. 8 Science Photo Library/Photolibrary Video/Getty Images; p. 10 Specialist Stock/RF Video+/Getty Images; p. 11 Jeff Rotman/The Image Bank/Getty Images; p. 14 Beyond Vision/Oxford Scientific Video/Getty Images; p. 17 Kim Briers/Shutterstock.com; p. 21 tagstiles.com - S. Gruene/Shutterstock.com; p. 22 by wildestanimal/Flickr/Getty Images.

Library of Congress Cataloging-in-Publication Data

Berne, Emma Carlson.
 Whale sharks: bulletproof! / by Emma Carlson Berne. — First edition.
    pages cm. — (Animal superpowers)
 Includes index.
 ISBN 978-1-4777-0749-4 (library binding) — ISBN 978-1-4777-0839-2 (pbk.) —
 ISBN 978-1-4777-0840-8 (6-pack)
 1. Whale shark—Juvenile literature. I. Title.
 QL638.95.R4B47 2014
 597.3'3—dc23
                                    2012046087

Manufactured in the United States of America

CPSIA Compliance Information: Batch #S13PK6: For Further Information contact Rosen Publishing, New York, New York at 1-800-237-9932

Contents

A Giant Fish

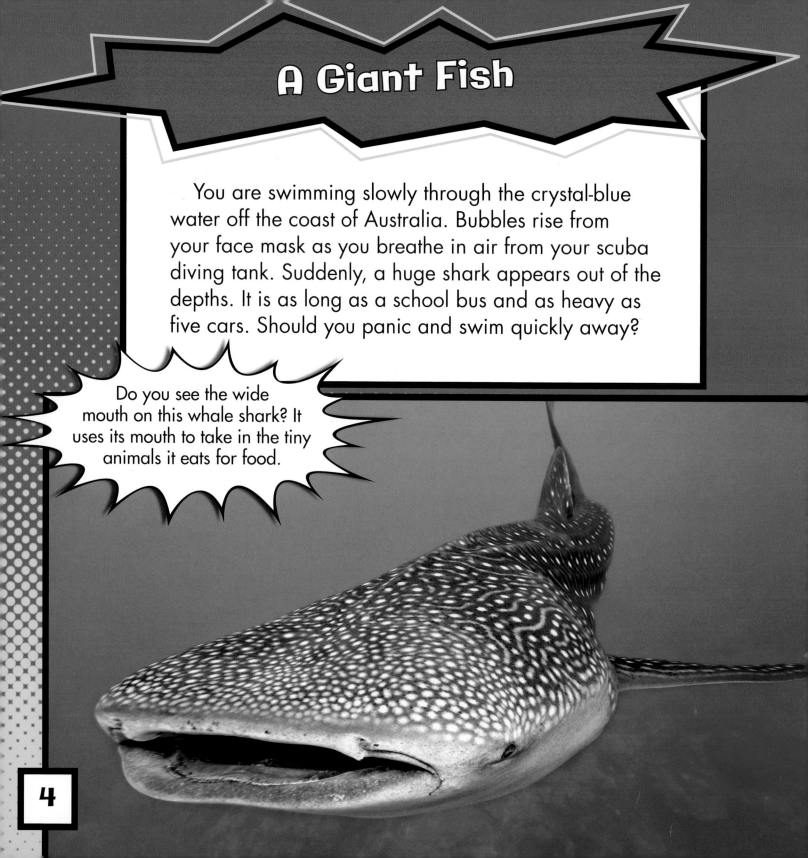

You are swimming slowly through the crystal-blue water off the coast of Australia. Bubbles rise from your face mask as you breathe in air from your scuba diving tank. Suddenly, a huge shark appears out of the depths. It is as long as a school bus and as heavy as five cars. Should you panic and swim quickly away?

Do you see the wide mouth on this whale shark? It uses its mouth to take in the tiny animals it eats for food.

There is no need. You are looking at a whale shark, an animal with some amazing superpowers.

What are some of this animal's superpowers? This gentle creature is the largest member of the shark family, the largest fish in the world, and one of the largest animals on the planet. It eats only the tiniest sea creatures, though. Let's learn more about this giant fish.

THE GIANT, GENTLE WHALE SHARK

Is It a Whale or a Shark?

Whale sharks take air from the water using gills. They do not have lungs, as mammals, such as whales and people, do.

A whale shark's name is confusing! Is this creature a whale or a shark? Luckily, there's an easy answer. A whale shark is a shark.

A shark is a fish and a whale is a **mammal**. Like all fish, a whale shark is **cold-blooded**. Whales and other mammals are **warm-blooded**.

6

BULLET-PROOF SKIN

How is a whale shark like Superman? Many people say that whale sharks have bullet-proof skin. While hopefully no one will test this out, these sharks have the thickest skin of any animal on the planet. It is 4 inches (10 cm) thick! The thickest skin on humans is only .05 inch (1.27 mm) thick.

The whale shark breathes underwater through **gills**. A whale breathes air through lungs, just as a person does. A whale shark does have a few features that some whales also have, though. It is huge and it sucks food through a filter in its mouth instead of using teeth.

Whales, such as this one, have to come to the top of the water to breathe.

7

Warm Water Lovers

Like most sharks, the whale shark lives in the salty water of the ocean. It likes warm water that is about 70 to 80° F (20–30° C). Plankton like this temperature, too, so the sharks can find plenty to eat.

The whale shark lives in the widest area of all sharks. Divers have seen whale sharks in the Atlantic, Pacific, and Indian Oceans. Whale sharks also **migrate**.

Here we can see the whale shark in shallow, warm waters.

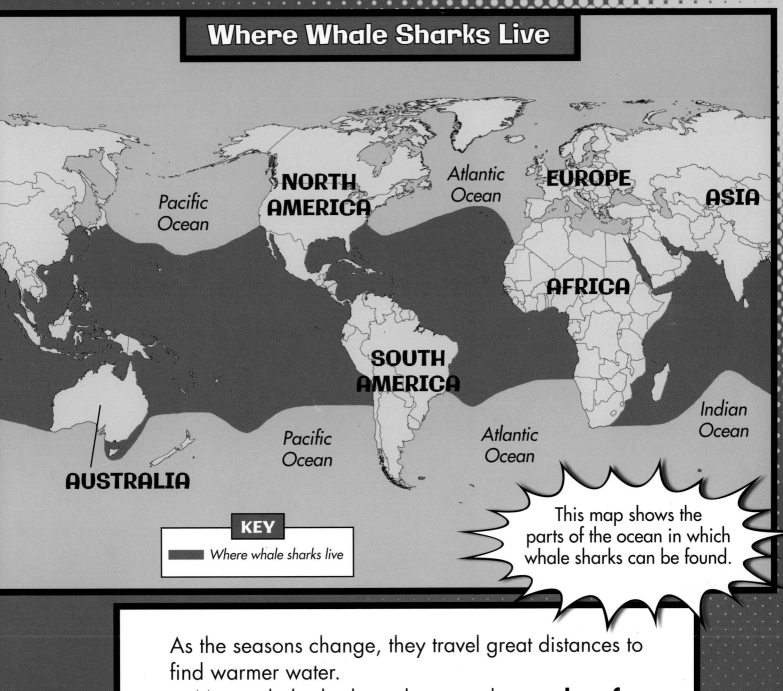

Where Whale Sharks Live

Pacific
Ocean

**NORTH
AMERICA**

Atlantic
Ocean

EUROPE

ASIA

AFRICA

**SOUTH
AMERICA**

Pacific
Ocean

Atlantic
Ocean

Indian
Ocean

AUSTRALIA

KEY
Where whale sharks live

This map shows the
parts of the ocean in which
whale sharks can be found.

As the seasons change, they travel great distances to
find warmer water.

Many whale sharks gather near the **coral reefs**
off the coast of western Australia each year. This
gives scientists a chance to study them more closely.

9

Gentle Giants

Whale sharks have wondrous bodies. As you already know, they are the largest of all sharks and one of the largest animals on Earth. The biggest whale shark ever measured was more than 40 feet (12 m) long and weighed 11 tons (10 t).

Whale sharks have tiny teeth. They don't even use their teeth for eating! Instead, they have filters in their gills to suck in plankton.

Whale sharks are known for their extra long tail fins.

10

Whale sharks have small eyes. Most scientists think that they cannot see very well. However, they have a superpowered sense of smell. They can smell tiny amounts of chemicals in the water. These traces lead them to their food.

Scientists think whale sharks' spots might help them blend in in the shallow waters where they spend a lot of time eating krill and other animals. Their huge mouths have lots of teeth, but they are tiny and not used for eating.

1 Whale sharks often carry hitchhikers with them. They are little fish called remoras. The remoras attach themselves with suckers to the shark's underside and eat **parasites** that live on the shark.

2 Whale sharks are known to be gentle to people. Scuba divers are sometimes able to hold on to a whale shark fin and get a ride underwater.

3 No one really knows how long whale sharks live, but scientists think it might be about 60 years. Some think they could live as long as 100 years.

4 Most scientists think a whale shark cannot have babies until it is about 30 years old.

5 The world population of whale sharks is in the hundreds of thousands. Whale sharks are a threatened species, though. This means that they could become **endangered** without protection.

6 Whale sharks are not very fast swimmers. They cruise underwater at between about 2 and 3 miles per hour (3–5 km/h). That's about the same speed as a person taking a stroll.

13

Yum, Plankton!

When a whale shark moves through the water with its mouth open wide like this, tiny sea creatures had better watch out. Whale sharks eat 46 pounds (21 kg) of krill and plankton daily.

Whale sharks eat small fish, **krill**, and plankton. Plankton are tiny animals that float in the water. When it is hungry, the whale shark opens its huge mouth and sucks in a lot of water. Then it blows the water out of its gills. The little fish, krill, and plankton get caught in the filters the whale shark has in its gills.

14

Krill are tiny shrimplike crustaceans, which serve as the food for countless animals, including birds, whales, and whale sharks. The largest krill are about the size of a paper clip.

Sometimes, a whale shark will swim straight up through a school of fish, then sink back down through the water with its mouth open. The water and fish are sucked right into the shark's mouth.

People Are the Predators

Whale sharks are lucky. Most animals have at least some **predators**. The whale shark has almost none, though. This is partly due to its enormous size and partly due to its incredibly thick skin. Other animals can't bite through it!

In some countries, whale sharks are hunted for their fins, meat, and oil. Due to falling numbers of these fish, though, fishing for them is banned in many places around the world.

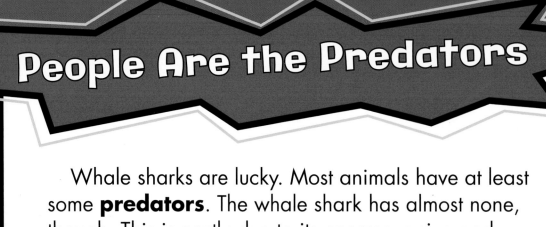

Sometimes, other sharks or large fish eat baby whale sharks. Scientists once found a baby whale shark in the belly of a fish called a marlin. Another time, they found one in the belly of a blue shark.

People are the biggest predators of whale sharks. Sharp boat propellers often wound the animals. In some parts of the world, they are hunted for their fins.

Orcas sometimes prey upon whale shark babies. Orcas are marine mammals that hunt in both cold and tropical waters around the world.

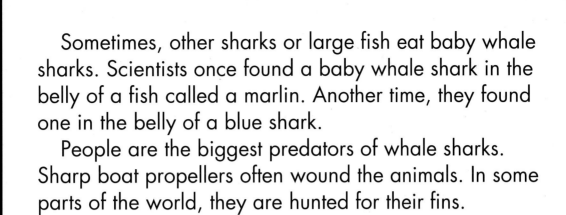

Making Whale Shark Babies

Scientists only discovered how whale sharks have babies under 20 years ago. Studying them in the wild is difficult and there aren't very many in aquariums.

Even though sharks are fish, some of them lay eggs, and others, such as the nurse shark, give birth to live babies. The whale shark combines both.

The female whale shark meets and **mates** with a male whale shark. Then she carries the fertilized eggs inside her body. The eggs hatch inside the mother, and then she births the live babies.

Whale sharks tend to be solitary, or like to live alone. Sometimes they can be seen near each other if there is a lot of food in one place. They also come together to mate.

19

This is a four-week-old whale shark that was born near the Galápagos Islands.

No one knows very much about baby whale sharks. Scientists have seen only one pregnant female. They have never seen babies actually being born. They know almost nothing about where the babies are born either.

In 2009, wildlife workers in the Philippines found a tiny baby whale shark tied to a stick near the shore. They released the baby into the open ocean. They guessed that the baby was probably born somewhere nearby. This was an important clue. Now scientists can see if that area of the ocean might be a **breeding ground** for whale sharks.

SUPERPOWERED SKIN

Sharks, including whale sharks, have amazingly sensitive skin. They actually use their skin to find fish to eat. When fish swim, their movements make little electric currents in the water. Sharks can feel these currents with special **pores** on their skin. Then they can easily follow the fish. Mmm, dinner!

Whale Sharks and Us

Even with their superhuge size and their superpowered skin, the whale shark needs our help. Most countries have banned whale shark hunting. People still do it, even though it is against the law. Whale sharks get caught in fishing nets and hurt by boats, too.

Scientists do their best to study these gentle giants, but we still don't know very much about them. These beautiful creatures are in danger of becoming extinct if we do not work to protect them.

Only aquariums with really large tanks can keep whale sharks. There are fewer than 20 whale sharks in aquariums worldwide. There are 4 of them living in the aquarium in Atlanta, Georgia.

Glossary

breeding ground (BREED-ing GROWND) A place where a certain kind of animal gives birth.

cold-blooded (KOHLD-bluh-did) Having a body heat that changes with the surrounding heat.

coral reefs (KOR-ul REEFS) Underwater hills of coral, which is hard matter made up of the bones of tiny sea animals.

endangered (in-DAYN-jerd) In danger of no longer existing.

gills (GILZ) Body parts that fish use for breathing.

krill (KRIL) Tiny sea animals.

mammal (MA-mul) A warm-blooded animal that has a backbone and hair, breathes air, and feeds milk to its young.

mates (MAYTS) Comes together to make babies.

migrate (MY-grayt) To move from one place to another.

parasites (PER-uh-syts) Living things that live in, on, or with other living things.

pores (PORZ) Tiny openings in the skin where liquid can pass through.

predators (PREH-duh-terz) Animals that kill other animals for food.

warm-blooded (WORM-bluh-did) Having a body heat that stays the same, no matter how warm or cold the surroundings are.

Index

A
air, 4, 7
Australia, 4, 9

C
coast, 4, 9
coral reefs, 9

F
family, 5
features, 7
filter(s), 7, 10, 14
fish, 5–6, 13–15,
    17–18, 21
food, 7, 11

G
gills, 7, 10, 14

K
krill, 14

L
lungs, 7

M
mammal(s), 6
mouth, 7, 14–15

N
name, 6

O
ocean(s), 8, 21

P
parasites, 13
pores, 21

S
skin, 7, 16, 21–22

T
teeth, 7, 10

W
whale(s), 6–7

Websites

Due to the changing nature of Internet links, PowerKids Press has developed an online list of websites related to the subject of this book. This site is updated regularly. Please use this link to access the list:
www.powerkidslinks.com/asp/shark/